Self-Love Workbook for Women

A Comprehensive Guide to Nurturing Self-Worth and Embracing Your Authentic Self

Laura Auster

Table of the Contents:

Chapter 1: Introduction to Self-Love 4

Chapter 2: The Journey of Self-Discovery 14

Chapter 3: Breaking the Chain of Negative Self-Talk 26

Chapter 4: Boundaries and Self-Care 43

Chapter 5: Dealing with Body Image and Self-Esteem 54

Chapter 6: Healing Past Wounds 58

Chapter 7: Embracing Imperfections 62

Chapter 8: Building Resilience 68

Chapter 9: The Role of Forgiveness in Self-Love 73

Chapter 10: Cultivating Gratitude 84

Chapter 11: Nurturing Healthy Relationships 89

Chapter 1: Introduction to Self-Love

In the world of psychology and wellness, the term 'self-love' has been used extensively, but what exactly does it mean? This chapter aims to unpack the concept of self-love and provide you with a clear understanding of its importance.

Defining Self-Love

The Essence of Self-Love

Self-love, at its core, refers to a deep and authentic regard for one's own well-being and happiness. This doesn't simply imply taking care of our basic needs, but extending love, respect, and compassion towards ourselves, much like how we would to a dear friend.

This self-regard forms the bedrock of our self-perception, the mirror through which we view ourselves. It's not about ignoring our faults or fostering an inflated ego, but instead acknowledging our complete self, with all our strengths and weaknesses, and accepting it wholeheartedly.

Love, Respect, and Kindness

Part of self-love involves treating ourselves kindly and with respect. This translates to not being excessively critical of our shortcomings or failures. Instead, we should cultivate a sense of patience and understanding towards our own mistakes, viewing them as opportunities for growth and learning rather than reflections of personal inadequacy.

Self-love also encourages us to stand up for ourselves and our needs, reinforcing the idea that we deserve respect and kindness, not just from others, but first and foremost from ourselves.

Inherent Worth

A central tenet of self-love is the recognition that our worth is inherent and doesn't depend on external factors. This means understanding that our value as individuals isn't determined by whether we meet societal expectations, how much approval we garner from others, the level of our achievements, or our physical appearance.

Too often, we tether our self-worth to these external elements, resulting in a fragile self-esteem that fluctuates based on outside validation. Self-love invites us to uncouple our worth from these external factors and to appreciate ourselves simply for who we are - unique individuals with our own journeys and stories.

The Relevance of Self-Love

Every aspect of our lives, from our mental health to our relationships, is touched by self-love. It's like the oxygen mask in an airplane emergency — we need to secure our own mask first before we can effectively help others. Similarly, nurturing self-love is essential before we can genuinely extend love and care to those around us.

Embracing self-love doesn't mean that we'll never experience self-doubt or criticism again, but it equips us with the resilience to confront these challenges with kindness and compassion towards ourselves. The journey towards self-love is a continuous process, and each step, no matter how small, contributes to fostering a more loving and harmonious relationship with ourselves.

Self-Love vs. Narcissism

Understanding Narcissism

Narcissism is a term that originates from Greek mythology, where a beautiful youth named Narcissus fell in love with his own reflection in a pool of water and couldn't tear himself away, leading to his downfall. In psychological terms, narcissism is characterized by an inflated sense of self-importance, an intense focus on oneself, and a lack of empathy for others. Narcissists often have a constant need for admiration and affirmation from others, and they tend to disregard the feelings and needs of the people around them.

The Thin Line

The line between self-love and narcissism can sometimes seem blurry, but there are key differences that distinguish the two. While self-love is about having a healthy level of respect and care for oneself, narcissism crosses over into the territory of self-obsession and disregard for others.

Key Differences

Here are a few crucial differences between self-love and narcissism:

- **Empathy:** Individuals who practice self-love also tend to have empathy for others, recognizing that everyone has their struggles and vulnerabilities. On the other hand, narcissists often struggle to empathize with others' feelings and needs, focusing primarily on their own.
- **Acknowledging Faults:** Self-love involves recognizing and accepting our flaws and understanding that we, like all humans, are a work in progress. Narcissists, however, are often unable to admit their mistakes and may blame others instead.
- **Validation:** While self-love cultivates a sense of self-worth that is independent of external validation, narcissists often rely heavily on approval and admiration from others to maintain their inflated self-image.
- **Respect for Others:** Self-love respects the boundaries and autonomy of others. In contrast, narcissism often disregards others' boundaries and needs, viewing them

only in terms of how they can serve the narcissist's interests.

Understanding the difference between self-love and narcissism is essential to promote healthy self-regard and avoid falling into patterns of narcissistic behavior. While self-love nourishes our psychological well-being and fosters healthier relationships, narcissism can lead to strained relationships and emotional distress for both the narcissist and those around them.

Components of Self-Love

Self-Acceptance

Self-acceptance is a cornerstone of self-love. It involves a genuine acknowledgment and acceptance of who we are at our core. This doesn't mean we deny our flaws or stop striving for improvement. Instead, it's about recognizing our strengths and weaknesses and embracing them as part of our unique human experience. When we practice self-acceptance, we learn to silence the harsh critic within us that undermines our self-worth and replace it with a compassionate voice that supports and nurtures us.

Self-Care

Self-care is another critical component of self-love. It entails taking care of our physical, emotional, and mental health. This might include activities like maintaining a balanced diet, getting regular exercise, ensuring we get enough sleep, participating in activities we enjoy, and spending time with loved ones. It also includes seeking professional help when needed, such as therapy or counseling. Self-care isn't just about indulgence but about making choices that sustain our long-term health and happiness.

Self-Compassion

Self-compassion involves extending compassion to ourselves when we make mistakes or go through difficult times, understanding that failure and struggle are parts of the universal human experience. Instead of punishing ourselves for our shortcomings, self-compassion encourages us to be understanding and patient. It involves recognizing our common humanity – the fact that we are not alone in our experiences of pain or failure, and such experiences are a part of being human.

Self-Respect

Self-respect is closely tied to self-love. It involves recognizing our own worth and insisting on being treated with respect and dignity. This can involve setting healthy boundaries in our relationships, asserting our needs and rights, and removing ourselves from harmful situations or relationships. When we respect ourselves, we set a standard for how we allow others to treat us.

Together, these components of self-love create a synergistic effect. By cultivating self-acceptance, self-care, self-compassion, and self-respect, we can develop a deep and lasting relationship with ourselves that fosters well-being and personal growth.

The Importance of Self-Love

Self-Love and Mental Health

Self-love has a profound impact on our mental health. Studies have shown that individuals who have high levels of self-love are less likely to suffer from mental health issues like anxiety, depression, and stress-related disorders. By accepting and caring for ourselves, we create a psychological buffer that can help us navigate the challenges of life with more resilience and flexibility.

Healthy Behaviors and Self-Love

When we practice self-love, we naturally gravitate towards behaviors that promote our well-being. This is because self-love engenders respect for our bodies and minds, leading us to make choices that support our overall health. We're more likely to engage in regular physical activity, eat a balanced diet, get adequate sleep, and seek medical attention when needed.

Self-Love and Relationships

Self-love sets the tone for how we allow others to treat us, which directly influences the quality of our relationships. When we value ourselves, we cultivate healthier, more fulfilling relationships because we're less likely to accept poor treatment or violation of our boundaries. Furthermore, self-love helps us navigate conflict with more grace, as we're more likely to communicate our feelings and needs effectively rather than reacting from a place of hurt or defensiveness.

The Journey of Self-Love

Self-love is not an overnight transformation, nor is it a destination we arrive at and then cease to move. Instead, it's an ongoing journey of discovery, acceptance, and growth. Some days it might be harder to love ourselves than others, and that's okay. The goal isn't to reach a state of perfect self-love, but rather to continually strive towards greater acceptance and compassion for ourselves.

Self-Reflective Activity

Understanding Your Relationship with Yourself

As we embark on this journey towards cultivating self-love, it's important to first understand our current relationship with ourselves. Take a moment to reflect on the following questions:

- How would you describe your relationship with yourself?
- What words or phrases come to mind when you think about how you treat yourself?

Be as honest as possible in your answers, and remember that this exercise is purely for self-reflection and growth. There's no need for judgement or criticism. Write down your thoughts in a journal or notebook.

Identifying Your Struggles

Next, take some time to reflect on which aspects of self-love you struggle with the most. This could involve questions like:

- Do you find it hard to accept your flaws?
- Do you struggle with setting boundaries in your relationships?
- Are you often critical of yourself, especially when you make mistakes or face challenges?
- Do you tend to ignore your needs or put others' needs before your own?

Again, write down your answers. Identifying our struggles is the first step towards addressing them.

Acknowledging Your Feelings

Lastly, take note of any feelings that arise during this self-reflection. You might experience a range of emotions, from discomfort and resistance to relief or sadness. These feelings are completely normal. Acknowledge them and allow yourself to feel them fully. Remember, self-compassion is a key aspect of self-love, and it starts with being kind to ourselves even when confronting difficult emotions.

Embracing the Journey

The journey towards self-love often involves delving into the less comfortable parts of ourselves, but each bit of self-awareness gained is a step towards developing a deeper, more compassionate relationship with ourselves. Celebrate this step you've taken in self-reflection – it's an essential part of your self-love journey. Hold onto your answers from this activity; as you progress through this book, you may find it helpful to revisit them and reflect on how your relationship with yourself evolves.

Chapter 2: The Journey of Self-Discovery

Introduction to Self-Discovery

Self-discovery is the process of gaining insight into one's character, feelings, motives, and desires. It's a journey into the deepest corners of our being, leading to a better understanding of who we are and what makes us tick. As such, self-discovery is a crucial aspect of cultivating self-love. The more we know ourselves, the better we can nurture a genuine sense of self-acceptance and appreciation.

What is Self-Discovery?

Self-discovery isn't about creating a new self but uncovering the real you that's always been there, beneath societal conditioning, expectations, and self-doubt. It's about stripping away the masks we wear and revealing our authentic selves. The process often involves exploring our strengths and weaknesses, understanding our passions

Why is Self-Discovery Important?

Self-discovery empowers us to live more authentically and fulfil our potential. By knowing our strengths, we can leverage them to achieve our goals. By acknowledging our weaknesses, we can develop strategies to address them. By understanding our passions, we can align our lives with what truly brings us joy.

And by facing our fears, we can make peace with them and reduce their hold on us.

Moreover, self-discovery fosters self-acceptance—a key component of self-love. When we truly know ourselves, we're more likely to accept and appreciate our unique qualities, rather than judging ourselves based on external standards or comparisons with others.

The Journey Ahead

The journey of self-discovery isn't always easy. It requires honesty, introspection, and courage to face aspects of ourselves we may have been avoiding. However, the rewards are immeasurable. Not only does self-discovery enhance our self-love, but it also enriches our relationships, increases our life satisfaction, and supports our personal and professional growth.

In this chapter, we'll guide you through various aspects of self-discovery, providing exercises and reflections to facilitate your journey. Remember, this process is deeply personal and unique to everyone—there's no right or wrong way to go about it. The most important thing is to approach it with an open mind, patience, and kindness towards yourself.

Understanding Your Strengths

What are Strengths?

Strengths are natural talents, abilities, skills, or traits that we excel in. They can range from interpersonal skills like empathy or leadership to personal attributes such as creativity, resilience, or discipline. They can also include specific competencies like writing, problem-solving, or public speaking. Importantly, our strengths contribute positively to our lives and those around us, helping us perform effectively and feel fulfilled.

Why Recognize Your Strengths?

Recognizing our strengths has several benefits. Firstly, it boosts our self-esteem and sense of self-worth. Understanding that we possess unique qualities that add value can improve our self-image and encourage self-love. Secondly, recognizing our strengths enables us to leverage them effectively in various life areas, such as our careers, personal growth, or relationships. Lastly, focusing on our strengths rather than dwelling on our weaknesses fosters a positive mindset, which contributes to better mental well-being.

Identifying Your Strengths

Identifying our strengths requires self-reflection and honesty. Some questions to consider might include:

- What tasks do you naturally excel at?
- What activities make you feel energized and fulfilled?

- What skills or qualities do others often compliment you on?

You might also consider using tools such as strengths assessment tests or feedback from people you trust to help identify your strengths.

Celebrating Your Strengths

Once we've identified our strengths, it's important to celebrate them. This doesn't mean bragging or developing a superiority complex, but rather, acknowledging and appreciating the value we bring. Celebrating our strengths could involve using them more often, developing them further, or simply allowing ourselves to feel proud of them.

Remember, recognizing and celebrating our strengths is not about comparing ourselves to others. Each of us is unique, with our own blend of strengths. The goal is to appreciate and embrace our individual strengths, contributing to our journey of self-love and self-acceptance.

Acknowledging Your Weaknesses

What are Weaknesses?

Weaknesses are areas where we may struggle or lack proficiency. These could be certain skills, habits, or personal traits. For example, someone might struggle with time management, be overly self-critical, or have difficulty expressing their feelings. Importantly, acknowledging our weaknesses is not an invitation to self-deprecation but a courageous step towards personal growth.

Why Acknowledge Your Weaknesses?

Recognizing our weaknesses is crucial for several reasons. Firstly, it fosters self-awareness, providing a more realistic and balanced understanding of ourselves. Secondly, acknowledging our weaknesses identifies areas for improvement and personal growth. Lastly, it helps us develop empathy and compassion for ourselves and others, recognizing that nobody is perfect and everyone has their struggles.

Identifying Your Weaknesses

Identifying your weaknesses requires honesty and introspection. Some guiding questions might include:

- What tasks or situations do you often find challenging?
- Are there any habits or traits you believe are holding you back?

- What feedback have you received from others about areas you could improve?

Remember, this exercise is not about dwelling on these weaknesses or using them to criticize yourself. It's about understanding yourself better and identifying areas for potential growth.

Treating Your Weaknesses with Kindness and Understanding

Once we've identified our weaknesses, the next step is to treat them with kindness and understanding. This means not berating ourselves for our flaws but recognizing that everyone has them, and they're part of what makes us human. Instead of viewing our weaknesses as permanent flaws, we can see them as areas for growth and development. This perspective shift fosters self-compassion, a crucial aspect of self-love.

Also, remember that acknowledging weaknesses doesn't mean obsessing over them. While it's important to work on our weaknesses, we should balance this by focusing on our strengths and the positive aspects of our personality. This balanced approach is crucial for cultivating self-love and a healthy self-image.

Discovering Your Passions

What are Passions?

Passions are intense interests or pursuits that fill us with joy, energy, and purpose. They could be activities, subjects, causes, or even relationships. Whether it's painting, learning about history, volunteering for a cause you believe in, or raising a family, passions make our hearts sing and often align with our core values.

Why Discover Your Passions?

Discovering your passions brings several benefits. Firstly, engaging in activities we're passionate about can boost our mood, reduce stress, and increase our overall life satisfaction. Secondly, our passions often guide us towards our life's purpose, helping us find meaningful careers or hobbies. Lastly, knowing what we're passionate about can help us connect with others who share similar interests, fostering meaningful relationships.

Identifying Your Passions

Identifying your passions may require some soul-searching. Here are a few questions to get you started:

- What activities make you lose track of time?
- Is there a cause you feel strongly about?
- What topics do you love learning about or discussing?
- Are there any dreams or goals you've always had but haven't pursued yet?

In addition to these questions, you can also look at your past experiences. Think about moments when you felt truly alive, engaged, and fulfilled - what were you doing? These moments can provide clues to your passions.

Living Your Passions

Once you've identified your passions, consider how you can incorporate them into your life. This could mean pursuing a career or hobby related to your passion, volunteering for a cause that matters to you, or simply dedicating more time to activities that bring you joy. Remember, living your passions is a key aspect of self-love - it's about honoring your authentic self and pursuing what genuinely makes you happy.

In the next section, we will explore fears and how they can often mask themselves as barriers to discovering and pursuing our passions. By acknowledging and addressing these fears, we pave the way to a life more closely aligned with our authentic selves.

Facing Your Fears

What are Fears?

Fears are emotional responses to perceived threats. They can be about specific situations, like fear of heights or public speaking, or more abstract and existential, like fear of failure, rejection, or being alone. While some fears can protect us from danger, others can limit our potential and prevent us from living our lives to the fullest.

Why Face Your Fears?

Facing your fears is crucial for several reasons. Firstly, it allows us to recognize and challenge the limiting beliefs that often accompany these fears. Secondly, by understanding our fears, we can develop strategies to manage them effectively, enabling us to pursue our passions and goals despite them. Lastly, facing our fears fosters courage, resilience, and personal growth – key elements in our journey of self-love and self-discovery.

Identifying Your Fears

Identifying your fears requires introspection and honesty. You might start by asking yourself:

- What situations or possibilities make you feel anxious or scared?
- Have you ever avoided a situation or decision due to fear?

- Can you recognize patterns in your fears? Do they relate to specific themes like rejection, failure, or uncertainty?

Remember, acknowledging your fears is not a sign of weakness. It's a brave act of self-awareness and the first step towards managing them effectively.

Managing Your Fears

Once we've identified our fears, the next step is learning how to manage them. This doesn't mean eliminating the fear entirely – which is often not possible or necessary – but rather learning to act despite it. This might involve:

- **Cognitive strategies:** Challenging the negative beliefs associated with your fears. For example, if you fear failure, remind yourself that everyone makes mistakes and that failure is often a stepping stone to success.
- **Behavioral strategies:** Gradually exposing yourself to the feared situation in a controlled and manageable way.
- **Emotional strategies:** Developing self-soothing techniques to manage the anxiety associated with your fears, such as deep breathing, mindfulness, or progressive muscle relaxation.

Remember, it's perfectly okay to seek professional help if your fears feel overwhelming. Therapists and counselors are trained to help people understand and manage their fears effectively.

By facing our fears, we take back control from them, empowering ourselves to live more authentically and lovingly towards ourselves.

Self-Reflective Activity

Strengths and Weaknesses Journaling

Take a quiet moment for yourself and start a journal entry. Start by listing your strengths. They could be talents, skills, positive traits, or anything you believe you excel at. Once you have a substantial list, write down a few instances where you've seen these strengths in action.

Next, move on to your weaknesses. This might be a bit harder, but remember, this is a safe space and this exercise is for your growth. List areas you'd like to improve on, along with instances where these have become apparent.

Revisit this list over time, adding to it as you continue to grow and learn about yourself.

Passion Exploration

For this activity, you need a piece of paper and a pen. Write "My Passions" at the top of the paper. Now, start jotting down activities, causes, or ideas that excite you, make you feel alive, or give you a sense of purpose. Don't overthink or judge what comes up.

Once you have your list, review it. Do you see any themes? Are you currently incorporating these passions into your life? How might you pursue these passions more actively?

Facing Your Fears

Write down your fears, however big or small they seem. For each fear, write about where you think it comes from and how it affects your life. Then, for each fear, write a counter statement that challenges it. For instance, if your fear is "I am afraid of failing," your counter statement could be "Every failure is a learning opportunity that brings me closer to success."

Remember, these activities are for you to explore yourself deeply. Don't rush through them. Take your time and be as honest with yourself as possible. You might discover things about yourself you didn't realize before, and that's what self-discovery is all about. The more we know ourselves, the better we can love ourselves.

Chapter 3: Breaking the Chain of Negative Self-Talk

The Power of Thoughts and Words

The Power of Thoughts

Our thoughts are an integral part of our inner world and exert a strong influence over our emotional state, decisions, and overall behavior. Every thought that crosses our mind has the potential to impact us, whether it's a fleeting, seemingly insignificant thought or a profound, lingering one.

When we entertain negative thoughts about ourselves, they can become deeply ingrained in our subconscious, forming a harmful narrative that undermines our self-esteem and confidence. This constant stream of self-deprecating thoughts can erode our mental well-being, making us more prone to feelings of anxiety, depression, and worthlessness.

The Power of Words

Our words, the tangible expressions of our thoughts, carry a similar weight. What we say to ourselves and about ourselves, whether out loud or in our minds, often becomes our reality. If we repeatedly tell ourselves that we are weak, inadequate, or unworthy, we begin to believe it, even if it's far from the truth.

Negative words create a self-fulfilling prophecy. They create a reality that reflects their negativity, not because they are inherently true, but because our belief in them changes our behavior, choices, and interactions in a way that makes them true.

Negative Self-Talk: A Detrimental Habit

Negative self-talk is a cycle of destructive self-dialogue that feeds our deepest insecurities and fears. It's the internal critic that continually undermines our efforts, no matter how small or big they are. It breeds self-doubt, diminishes our self-esteem, and skews our perception of self, often leading us to form an image of ourselves that is distorted and negatively biased.

Understanding this powerful influence that thoughts and words have over us is the first step towards breaking free from the damaging cycle of negative self-talk. As we move forward, we'll delve into how to identify and counteract these harmful narratives.

The Impact of Negative Self-Talk

Impact on Mental Health

Negative self-talk creates a breeding ground for anxiety, depression, and stress-related disorders. By continually telling ourselves that we are not good enough, we foster feelings of worthlessness and hopelessness. This perpetual self-devaluation can lead to a pervasive sense of sadness and loss of interest, hallmark symptoms of depression. Simultaneously, the constant worry about our inadequacies can trigger anxiety, keeping us in a state of heightened stress and worry.

Impact on Personal Development and Success

Negative self-talk also has a profound impact on our personal and professional development. It feeds our self-doubt, making us question our capabilities and worth. This can lead to procrastination, avoidance, and missed opportunities as we hold ourselves back out of fear of failure or rejection. We might even sabotage our success, believing we don't deserve it.

Impact on Relationships

Our relationship with ourselves sets the tone for all our other relationships. If we're continually criticizing and belittling ourselves through negative self-talk, we're likely to carry this behavior into our relationships. This can manifest as being overly critical of others, being defensive, or even pushing others away due to feelings of unworthiness. Alternatively, it could lead to accepting poor treatment from others because we don't believe we deserve better.

Impact on Physical Health

Often overlooked is the impact of negative self-talk on physical health. Chronic stress, fueled by negative self-talk, can lead to a range of physical health issues, including heart disease, digestive problems, sleep disturbances, and a weakened immune system.

The Science Behind Thoughts and Words

Negativity Bias

Our brains are wired to prioritize negative information due to a phenomenon known as the negativity bias. This is an evolutionary adaptation designed to keep us safe by helping us remember and learn from negative experiences so we can avoid them in the future. While beneficial for survival, this bias can lead to a tendency to focus excessively on negative thoughts and experiences and underestimate or even overlook positive ones.

Neuroplasticity and Negative Self-Talk

Neuroplasticity is the brain's ability to reorganize itself by forming new neural connections throughout life. While this ability is vital for learning and adaptation, it also means that repeated negative self-talk can lead to strengthened neural pathways associated with negativity, essentially wiring our brain to default to these patterns. The more we engage in negative self-talk, the stronger these neural pathways become, making it more difficult to break the habit of negative thinking.

Impact of Negative Self-Talk on Brain and Body

Persistent negative self-talk can also trigger a chronic stress response, leading to the release of stress hormones such as cortisol. Over time, high cortisol levels can lead to a host of health issues, including sleep disturbances, weight gain, heart disease, and a weakened immune system. Moreover, chronic stress can impair the brain's ability to function correctly, impacting memory, mood, and cognition.

The Good News: The Power of Positive Change

While the science behind negative self-talk may seem daunting, it also provides a roadmap for positive change. Just as negative thoughts can strengthen harmful neural pathways, positive thoughts can forge new, healthier ones. This means that by replacing negative self-talk with positive affirmations and self-compassion, we can rewire our brain towards more positive thinking patterns.

Identifying Negative Self-Talk

Forms of Negative Self-Talk

Negative self-talk comes in many forms, each characterized by a specific type of distorted thinking. Recognizing these patterns is the first step towards challenging and changing them.

Filtering

Filtering is a cognitive distortion where you magnify the negative aspects of a situation and filter out all of the positive ones. For instance, you may receive many compliments on a presentation, but focus only on the one minor constructive criticism you received.

Personalizing

When you personalize, you tend to blame yourself for anything that goes wrong, even if you're not directly responsible. For example, if a group project at work doesn't go well, you assume that it's your fault, ignoring other contributing factors.

Catastrophizing

Catastrophizing involves anticipating the worst in every situation. You might turn minor setbacks or mistakes into major catastrophes in your mind. If you make a small mistake at work, you may start thinking that you're going to get fired.

Polarizing

Polarizing, or 'black-and-white thinking,' involves seeing things as only good or bad, perfect or terrible, with no in-between. If you don't perform perfectly in some area, you may see yourself as a total failure.

Recognizing Negative Self-Talk

Identifying negative self-talk involves paying close attention to your inner dialogue. It can be helpful to keep a thought journal, noting down negative thoughts as they come up, along with the situation you were in when they occurred. This will help you identify patterns and triggers for negative self-talk, as well as the specific forms your negative self-talk tends to take.

Strategies to Overcome Negative Self-Talk

Challenging Negative Self-Talk

Once you've identified your patterns of negative self-talk, the next step is to challenge these thoughts. This involves examining them critically and asking yourself whether they are truly accurate or helpful. Some questions to ask yourself might include: Is this thought based on facts or assumptions? Is there another way to look at this situation? Is this thought helping me or hindering me?

Replacing Negative Self-Talk with Positive Affirmations

After challenging your negative self-talk, aim to replace it with positive affirmations. These are positive statements about yourself or your situation that help you maintain a positive outlook. The key is to make sure these affirmations are realistic and based on truth. For example, instead of telling yourself, "I can't do this," you might say, "I can handle this challenge because I've handled difficult situations before."

Mindfulness and Self-Talk

Mindfulness involves staying present and fully engaged in the current moment. By practicing mindfulness, you can become more aware of your self-talk as it occurs, allowing you to recognize and challenge negative thoughts more effectively. Mindfulness techniques might include meditation, focused breathing, or even just taking a moment to observe your surroundings and physical sensations.

Self-Compassion in Self-Talk

Cultivating self-compassion is another powerful way to combat negative self-talk. This involves treating yourself with the same kindness and understanding you would offer to a friend. When you notice negative self-talk, remind yourself that everyone makes mistakes and faces challenges, and that it's okay not to be perfect.

Seeking Support

Sometimes, negative self-talk can be a symptom of deeper mental health issues, such as depression or anxiety. If your negative self-talk is causing significant distress or if you're finding it difficult to manage on your own, it might be helpful to seek support from a mental health professional. They can provide you with additional strategies and treatments to manage negative self-talk and improve your mental health.

Remember, breaking the chain of negative self-talk is a journey, not an instant change. It takes time and practice, but every step you take towards more positive and compassionate self-talk is a significant step towards greater self-love.

Mindfulness and Awareness

The Role of Mindfulness

Mindfulness is a mental state achieved by focusing one's awareness on the present moment, calmly acknowledging and accepting feelings, thoughts, and bodily sensations. When it comes to self-talk, mindfulness can play an invaluable role. By becoming more mindful, we can catch negative self-talk in its early stages, acknowledge its presence, and decide not to let it dictate our emotions or behavior.

Practicing Mindfulness Meditation

Mindfulness meditation is a powerful tool for cultivating this type of awareness. This practice involves sitting comfortably, focusing on your breath, and bringing your mind's attention to the present without drifting into concerns about the past or future. It doesn't necessarily mean emptying the mind, but rather observing thoughts and feelings without judgment. This non-judgmental observation can help you recognize patterns of negative self-talk without getting swept up in them.

Regular Thought Check-Ins

Regular thought check-ins can also contribute to greater mindfulness and awareness. These are intentional moments of reflection throughout the day where you tune into your thoughts. You might ask yourself: What am I thinking right now? How am I talking to myself about the current situation? Am I falling into patterns of negative self-talk?

By regularly checking in with your thoughts, you can catch instances of negative self-talk early, challenge them, and redirect your thoughts in a more positive direction.

Mindfulness in Everyday Activities

In addition to formal meditation and regular thought check-ins, mindfulness can be practiced during everyday activities. For instance, you can practice mindfulness while eating, walking, or even washing dishes. This involves fully immersing yourself in the activity, paying attention to the sensory details, and observing your thoughts and feelings as they arise. By doing so, you can enhance your overall mindfulness and become more attuned to instances of negative self-talk.

Remember, developing mindfulness takes time and practice, but the benefits to your mental wellbeing and ability to manage negative self-talk are substantial.

Challenging Negative Thoughts

Assessing Accuracy

Our thoughts are not always a reflection of reality. Often, they can be influenced by our emotions, biases, or past experiences. When you catch yourself in a loop of negative self-talk, ask yourself: "Is this thought accurate? Is it a fact, or is it an interpretation influenced by my current mood or past experiences?" It can be helpful to write down your thoughts and look at them objectively.

Looking for Evidence

After assessing the accuracy of your thought, look for evidence that supports or disputes it. For instance, if your negative self-talk tells you that you're not good at anything, consider the skills you've developed, the tasks you've completed successfully, and the compliments you've received. This evidence can help you realize that the negative self-talk doesn't hold up to scrutiny.

Reframing Thoughts

Once you've challenged the accuracy of your thoughts and looked for evidence, it's time to reframe the negative self-talk. Reframing involves changing the way you interpret a situation, shifting from a negative perspective to a more positive or neutral one. For example, instead of saying "I always mess up," you could reframe it to "I made a mistake this time, but I've succeeded before and I can learn from this."

Practicing Self-Compassion

As you work on challenging and reframing your thoughts, remember to practice self-compassion. Avoid being too hard on yourself if negative thoughts still arise. It takes time to change thought patterns, and it's natural to slip back into old habits. Remind yourself that you're making progress and that each step, no matter how small, is a step in the right direction.

Challenging negative self-talk is a critical skill in your journey towards self-love. As you cultivate this skill, you'll find that your thoughts become less of a barrier to your happiness and more of a source of self.

Positive Affirmations

The Power of Positive Affirmations

Positive affirmations are simple, positive statements that describe a desired situation or goal, and they're used to challenge and overcome self-sabotaging and negative thoughts. When they're repeated regularly and believed in, they can start to make positive changes in your mindset and your life. They can help you maintain a positive self-image and outlook on life, even in the face of challenges and setbacks.

Creating Your Own Affirmations

Creating your own affirmations can be a powerful exercise because it allows you to tailor affirmations to your individual needs and circumstances. They should be personal, positive, present-tense statements. For instance, instead of saying, "I will not let fear dictate my decisions," you could say, "I make decisions based on courage and wisdom." The affirmation should feel uplifting and empowering to you.

How to Use Affirmations

Integrate affirmations into your daily routine. You could recite them in the morning to set a positive tone for the day, or in the evening to keep your subconscious mind focused on positive thoughts as you sleep. You could also use them in the moment to combat negative self-talk.

Remember to say them with conviction and belief. If it feels awkward or uncomfortable at first, remember that you're challenging long-held beliefs and that it will get easier with time.

The Potential of Positive Affirmations

While positive affirmations are not a magic solution and won't bring about changes overnight, they can play a significant part in shifting your mindset towards self-love and positivity. When used in conjunction with other strategies, like challenging negative thoughts and practicing mindfulness, they can be powerful tools in breaking the cycle of negative self-talk.

Seeking Professional Help

When to Seek Help

While many of us engage in negative self-talk from time to time, when these negative thoughts become pervasive, constant, and start to interfere with our daily life, relationships, and overall wellbeing, it may be time to seek professional help. Persistent negative self-talk can be a symptom of mental health conditions like depression or anxiety disorders.

The Role of Therapists and Counselors

Therapists and counselors are trained professionals who can provide strategies and tools to combat negative self-talk. They can guide you through the process of understanding and reprogramming your thought patterns. Therapy can provide a safe space to explore the roots of your negative self-talk, whether they stem from past experiences, ingrained beliefs, or coping mechanisms.

Different Types of Therapy

Different types of therapy can help with negative self-talk. Cognitive Behavioral Therapy (CBT) is a type of psychotherapy that helps you become aware of inaccurate or negative thinking so you can view challenging situations more clearly and respond to them more effectively. Acceptance and Commitment Therapy (ACT) is another approach that teaches you how to accept and observe your thoughts without getting entangled in them.

Taking the First Step

The first step towards seeking professional help can be daunting, but it's an important and brave step towards self-love and improved mental health. Start by researching therapists in your local area or online platforms that offer remote counseling. Look for professionals who specialize in dealing with the issues you're facing. Remember, it's completely okay to seek help, and doing so is an act of self-love.

Self-Reflective Activity

Identifying Your Patterns of Negative Self-Talk

In this exercise, take a moment to reflect on the negative phrases you often tell yourself. Do they center around a particular aspect of your life or your personality? Do you notice any patterns in the type of negative self-talk, such as catastrophizing or personalizing? Write these phrases down and note the situations that usually trigger them.

Challenging Negative Thoughts

After you've identified some of your common negative self-talk phrases, try to challenge them. Next to each negative phrase you've written, write a counter-argument. This could be evidence that contradicts the negative statement or a more balanced thought that acknowledges both your strengths and areas for improvement.

Crafting Positive Affirmations

Now, try transforming the negative phrases you've written into positive affirmations. For example, if your negative self-talk says, "I always mess up," you could write, "I learn and grow from my mistakes." Write these affirmations on post-it notes and stick them around your living space as a constant reminder.

Reflection and Forward Planning

Finally, reflect on this process. How did it feel to challenge your negative thoughts and create positive affirmations? Understand that this practice takes time and consistency. Create a plan for incorporating these strategies into your daily life. This could be setting aside a few minutes each day to practice mindfulness, repeating your affirmations every morning, or scheduling regular check-ins with yourself to notice any negative self-talk.

Remember, the goal of this activity and all exercises in this book is not to achieve perfection, but to foster self-love and improve your relationship with yourself. You're already on the right path by undertaking this work. Keep going, and celebrate every step you take towards self-love.

Chapter 4: Boundaries and Self-Care

Introduction to Boundaries and Self-Care

Boundaries are like invisible lines that we draw around ourselves to define where we end and where others begin. They represent our values, preferences, needs, and responsibilities, and serve to protect us from being violated by others – both physically and emotionally. They help us clearly communicate what we are and are not comfortable with, enabling us to maintain our autonomy and self-respect.

Moreover, setting healthy boundaries is an act of self-care and self-love. When we establish boundaries, we are essentially acknowledging our self-worth and taking steps to protect our mental, emotional, and physical well-being. We are also helping others understand how we want to be treated.

Understanding Personal Boundaries

Personal boundaries are unique to each individual, acting as guidelines, rules, or limits that a person identifies as non-negotiable in their relationships. These boundaries can be related to physical space, emotional interactions, and intellectual thoughts and ideas. Understanding the different types of boundaries is the first step in setting ones that cater to your specific needs.

1. **Physical boundaries**: These pertain to personal space, physical touch, and privacy. Everyone has different comfort levels when it comes to how close they allow others to get, whether or not they are comfortable with physical affection, and what they consider private.
2. **Emotional boundaries**: These relate to your feelings. They help you distinguish your emotions from someone else's. Emotional boundaries might also involve identifying how much emotional energy you are willing to absorb from others and protecting yourself from being emotionally manipulated or used.
3. **Mental boundaries**: These are tied to your thoughts, values, opinions, and beliefs. They involve respect for your ideas and thoughts, as well as the right to express them without fear of ridicule or dismissal.

A clear understanding of these different types of boundaries allows you to identify and express what you are comfortable with and what you are not in various areas of your life. This clarity is essential in maintaining your self-identity and ensuring your interactions with others are respectful and considerate of your personal boundaries.

The Importance of Personal Boundaries

Personal boundaries are integral to our overall wellbeing and healthy relationships. Here are some reasons why they are so crucial:

1. **Preserve Self-Identity**: Boundaries help define us as individuals, separating our feelings, thoughts, and needs from those of others. They ensure we maintain our individuality even in the context of close relationships.
2. **Protect Emotional Health**: Boundaries safeguard our emotional space, preventing us from absorbing or taking responsibility for other people's feelings and problems. They empower us to say 'no' when we need to without feeling guilty or selfish.
3. **Foster Autonomy**: Healthy boundaries enable us to express our needs and wants openly, fostering a sense of autonomy. They give us the freedom to make decisions that align with our personal values and aspirations.
4. **Promote Respect**: When we set clear boundaries, we communicate our self-worth to others. This signals how we expect to be treated, fostering mutual respect in our relationships.
5. **Prevent Burnout**: By setting boundaries, we manage our energy and time effectively, avoiding overcommitment and subsequent burnout. They allow us to allocate time for rest and self-care, which are integral for maintaining our physical, emotional, and mental wellbeing.
6. **Support Healthy Relationships**: Clear boundaries create an understanding and expectation in relationships, reducing the chances of conflict and misunderstanding. They create a balance of give-and-take, which is critical for sustaining healthy, fulfilling relationships.

How to Set Personal Boundaries

Creating healthy personal boundaries is a self-care practice that not only safeguards your well-being but also allows you to build stronger relationships. Here's how to go about setting these boundaries:

1. **Self-awareness**: First and foremost, you need to understand your feelings, needs, and values. What makes you feel uncomfortable or overwhelmed? What do you need to feel respected and safe? What aligns with your values? Reflection and journaling can be helpful tools in this process.

2. **Define Your Boundaries**: Once you understand your needs, you can start defining your boundaries. These will be unique to you and can span various areas of your life – from work and social engagements to personal relationships.

3. **Communicate Clearly**: Healthy boundaries need to be communicated clearly and assertively to be effective. Make your expectations known, express your feelings honestly, and do so in a respectful manner. Remember, it's okay to say 'no'.

4. **Practice Consistency**: Setting boundaries isn't a one-time event. It requires consistent reinforcement. If a boundary is crossed, communicate your discomfort and reaffirm your boundary. Over time, this consistency will make it easier for you and others to respect your boundaries.

5. **Seek Support**: Setting and maintaining boundaries can be challenging, especially if you're not used to it. Don't hesitate to seek support from trusted friends, family, or a professional counselor or therapist. They can provide valuable guidance and reinforcement.

6. **Self-Care and Self-Compassion**: Understand that it's okay if your boundaries are tested or crossed occasionally. The important thing is to treat yourself with kindness and compassion and continue to work on establishing and maintaining your boundaries. After all, they are crucial for your well-being and self-love journey.

Nurturing Self-Care through Boundaries

Boundaries and self-care are deeply interlinked. In fact, setting healthy boundaries is a form of self-care as it safeguards our mental, emotional, and physical well-being. Here's how boundaries can facilitate self-care:

1. **Preserving Energy**: Boundaries prevent us from overextending ourselves, helping conserve our mental and emotional energy. This energy can then be channeled into activities that nurture our wellbeing, such as hobbies, relaxation, or mindfulness practices.

2. **Creating Space for Self-Care**: Boundaries ensure we have the time and space necessary for self-care. This can include setting a boundary around taking regular breaks during the workday, having 'me time' each day, or maintaining a work-life balance.

3. **Supporting Emotional Health**: By setting boundaries around negative or toxic influences, we protect our emotional health. This support allows us to engage more fully in self-care practices that nurture positive emotions and mental health.

4. **Cultivating Self-Respect**: The act of setting and enforcing boundaries can boost our self-esteem and self-respect. It reaffirms our worth and reminds us that our needs and feelings are important.

Now, here are a few tips for nurturing self-care within your boundaries:

1. **Establish Self-Care Routines**: Once you have your boundaries in place, establish routines that prioritize self-care. This could include a morning routine that sets a positive tone for the day, regular exercise, or an evening relaxation routine.

2. **Practice Mindfulness**: Mindfulness helps us stay tuned into our needs and feelings. Regularly check in with yourself. How are you feeling? What do you need? This awareness can guide your self-care practices.

3. **Prioritize Activities You Enjoy**: Make time for activities that bring you joy and relaxation. These activities can replenish your energy and serve as a reward for maintaining your boundaries.

4. **Seek Balance**: Self-care is about balance. While it's important to take care of your physical health, also consider your mental and emotional health. This might

involve balancing time spent on work with time for relaxation and fun, or balancing social activities with time for solitude.

Remember, the aim of setting boundaries is not to isolate yourself, but to create a healthier relationship with yourself and others. When established and maintained properly, boundaries can greatly enhance your self-care routine and overall well-being.

Self-Reflective Activity

In this concluding section, we will guide you through a series of self-reflective activities designed to help you identify, establish, and enforce your personal boundaries. Remember, creating and maintaining boundaries is an ongoing process that requires self-awareness, assertiveness, and patience.

Activity 1: Identifying Current Boundaries

Reflect on your existing boundaries. Consider your relationships, work, and personal time. Ask yourself:

1. What boundaries have you already set in place?
2. How effective are these boundaries?
3. How do you feel when these boundaries are respected? What about when they are crossed?

Activity 2: Identifying Boundary Needs

Think about areas in your life where you feel stressed, overwhelmed, or taken advantage of. This might indicate a need for stronger or more explicit boundaries. Ask yourself:

1. In what situations do you often feel uncomfortable or drained?
2. Are there relationships where you feel your needs are not being respected?
3. Are there specific times or places where you feel you need more space or privacy?

Activity 3: Setting New Boundaries

For the areas you've identified in Activity 2, consider what new boundaries you might establish. Remember, boundaries should be explicit, reasonable, and clearly communicated. Ask yourself:

1. What specific actions or behaviors will you no longer tolerate?
2. How can you clearly communicate these boundaries to others?
3. What will you do if these boundaries are not respected?

Activity 4: Nurturing Self-Care through Boundaries

Now, consider how you can incorporate self-care into your boundaries. Reflect on your needs and what brings you joy and relaxation. Ask yourself:

1. How can you create time and space for self-care in your daily routine?
2. What activities or practices nurture your well-being?
3. How can you ensure these self-care practices are respected and prioritized?

As you go through these activities, remember that your needs and well-being are important. Establishing and maintaining boundaries is a self-affirming act of self-love and self-respect. Take your time, be patient with yourself, and make adjustments as needed. You're taking important steps toward a healthier, more balanced life.

The Importance of Self-Care for Physical, Emotional, and Mental Wellbeing

Self-care is an integral part of maintaining and improving our overall wellbeing. It refers to the conscious act of engaging in activities that promote physical, emotional, and mental health. Despite its importance, self-care often gets overlooked in our busy lives. Here's why it's essential:

1. **Physical wellbeing:** Regular self-care activities like exercising, eating a balanced diet, ensuring enough sleep, and maintaining good hygiene can greatly enhance our physical health, providing us with more energy and boosting our immune system.

2. **Emotional wellbeing:** Self-care activities like mindfulness, meditation, journaling, or simply spending time doing things we enjoy can help manage stress, foster emotional intelligence, and improve our mood.

3. **Mental wellbeing:** Regular self-care can help prevent mental health conditions like depression and anxiety. Even simple activities like reading, learning something new, or engaging in a hobby can stimulate our brains, enhancing cognitive function and mental resilience.

Incorporating regular self-care activities into our daily lives can significantly improve our overall wellbeing, making us more resilient, happy, and productive.

Activity: Creating a Personal Self-Care Plan

Creating a personal self-care plan can help ensure that you consistently prioritize your wellbeing. Here's a step-by-step guide on how you can create one:

Step 1: Identify what self-care activities you enjoy: These should be activities that you look forward to and that enhance your physical, emotional, or mental wellbeing. Examples can be reading a book, going for a run, practicing yoga, or even having a quiet cup of coffee.

Step 2: Evaluate your current self-care routine: Reflect on your current routine. How often do you engage in self-care activities? Are there times where you feel overly stressed or burned out? Use these insights to identify where you can make improvements.

Step 3: Set realistic self-care goals: Based on your evaluation, set some goals for your self-care routine. Be realistic and considerate of your existing commitments. Your goal could be as simple as "spend 15 minutes each day practicing mindfulness" or "exercise three times per week."

Step 4: Create a schedule: Once you have your goals, create a schedule. Decide when you'll engage in each self-care activity, considering when you'll be most likely to follow through.

Step 5: Monitor and adjust your plan: Regularly check in on your self-care plan. If you find you're not keeping up with your schedule or not enjoying certain activities, make adjustments. The goal is to create a plan that you enjoy and can sustain over the long term.

Remember, self-care isn't selfish; it's a necessary part of maintaining your wellbeing. By creating a personal self-care plan, you're prioritizing your health and happiness, which is a vital aspect of self-love.

Chapter 5: Dealing with Body Image and Self-Esteem

Understanding the Link Between Body Image and Self-Esteem

Body image and self-esteem are intricately linked. Body image refers to how we perceive our physical selves - our bodies. It's not just about what we see in the mirror, but also how we feel about our bodies - our size, shape, and physical appearance in general. Self-esteem, on the other hand, is how we value and perceive ourselves overall, not just our physical appearance.

Positive body image and self-esteem are crucial for overall health and wellbeing. When we feel good about our bodies, we're more likely to have a positive outlook on ourselves and life in general. Conversely, a negative body image can lead to low self-esteem, affecting our mental and emotional health.

It's important to remember that our body image and self-esteem are shaped by various factors, including societal and cultural standards, media influences, and interpersonal relationships. Recognizing these influences can be the first step in fostering a more positive body image and, in turn, improving self-esteem.

Strategies to Develop a Positive Body Image and Improve Self-Esteem

Improving body image and self-esteem requires a conscious effort and involves a range of strategies, some of which include:

Practice Self-Acceptance

Accepting your body as it is can be a powerful step towards improving body image. This doesn't mean ignoring or neglecting your health, but rather, it's about appreciating your body for what it is and what it can do.

Challenge Negative Thoughts

Negative thoughts about your body can be detrimental to both body image and self-esteem. By challenging these thoughts, and replacing them with positive or neutral ones, you can start to shift your perception of your body and yourself.

Limit Media Exposure

Media often presents unrealistic standards of beauty that can contribute to negative body image. Limiting exposure to such media and following body-positive accounts can help foster a healthier and more realistic view of bodies.

Practice Self-Care

Taking care of your physical health through regular exercise and a balanced diet can enhance your body image. Remember, this isn't about changing your body to fit a certain ideal but about caring for and respecting your body because it's yours.

Seek Professional Help

If negative body image and low self-esteem are causing significant distress or leading to unhealthy behaviors, it may be helpful to seek professional help. Therapists and counselors can provide strategies and support to help improve body image and self-esteem.

Activity: Body Positivity and Self-Esteem Journaling

Journaling can be a powerful tool for fostering body positivity and improving self-esteem. It can help you identify negative thought patterns, focus on the things you appreciate about your body, and track your progress as you journey towards a more positive body image and higher self-esteem.

Identifying Negative Thought Patterns

Start by journaling about your current thoughts and feelings about your body. Note any patterns of negative self-talk or body criticism. You might write down thoughts that come up throughout the day or reflections on how you feel about your body in general.

Focusing on Appreciation

Next, make a list of things you appreciate about your body. This could include physical attributes, abilities, or the way your body supports you in your daily life. Try to focus on what your body does rather than how it looks.

Challenging Negative Thoughts

Whenever you notice a negative thought about your body, write it down, then challenge it. Ask yourself if the thought is really true, if it's helpful, or if it's based on unrealistic standards. Try to replace the negative thought with a more positive or neutral one.

Tracking Progress

Use your journal to track your progress over time. Note any changes in your thoughts or feelings about your body, any improvements in your self-esteem, or any moments when you felt particularly positive about your body.

Remember, this is a personal journey, and progress might be slow sometimes. Be patient with yourself, and celebrate every step you take towards a more positive body image and higher self-esteem.

Chapter 6: Healing Past Wounds

Introduction to Healing Past Wounds

The journey towards self-love often involves confronting and healing past wounds. These may stem from difficult experiences, painful relationships, or mistakes we believe we've made. In this chapter, we will delve into the process of recognizing and accepting past hurts, releasing their grip on our present, and healing to move forward towards a more self-loving future.

Recognizing and Accepting Past Hurts

Recognizing past hurts is the first step towards healing them. This involves acknowledging the pain you experienced, understanding how it impacted you, and accepting that it is a part of your past. It's important to approach this process with self-compassion, recognizing that everyone carries some wounds from their past.

The Role of Acceptance in Healing

Acceptance is a powerful tool in healing past wounds. It doesn't mean condoning what happened or dismissing your feelings about it, but rather acknowledging that it did occur. Acceptance allows you to stop fighting or ignoring the pain and start focusing on how to heal from it.

Strategies for Recognizing and Accepting Past Hurts

This section will provide strategies and exercises to help you recognize and accept your past hurts. This might include reflection activities, writing exercises, mindfulness practices, or guided visualizations.

Remember, this process can be challenging, and it's okay to seek support from trusted friends, family, or professionals. Your journey towards healing is unique to you, and it's essential to honor your pace and process.

Techniques for Healing and Moving Forward

After recognizing and accepting past hurts, the next step is to start the healing process. This involves developing self-compassion, making peace with the past, and fostering resilience to move forward.

Cultivating Self-Compassion

Self-compassion is key in the healing process. This means treating yourself with the same kindness and understanding you would offer to a friend in pain. Self-compassion can help you process your past hurts without self-judgment or self-blame.

Making Peace with the Past

To heal, you'll need to make peace with your past. This doesn't mean forgetting what happened, but rather letting go of its hold on your present and future. You might find practices like forgiveness (of yourself and others), mindfulness, and perspective-shifting helpful in this process.

Fostering Resilience

Resilience is the capacity to recover from difficulties, and it's an essential element of healing. By developing resilience, you can learn to navigate future challenges with strength and grace. Techniques to foster resilience might include building a supportive network, developing healthy coping mechanisms, focusing on your strengths, and nurturing a positive outlook.

Practical Techniques for Healing

In this section, we will explore practical techniques for healing, such as journaling, meditation, creative expression, physical activity, therapy, and more. You will be guided to find what techniques work best for you and how to incorporate them into your healing process.

Remember, everyone's healing journey is different. There's no set timeline or "right" way to heal. The important thing is that you're taking steps towards healing and self-love, no matter how small.

Activity: Healing Letter Writing

One powerful way to facilitate healing is through writing. Specifically, writing a letter to your past self, your current self, or even to someone else who was involved in your past hurt can be an effective therapeutic exercise. This method is a form of expressive writing that can help you process your emotions, gain perspective, and give voice to your experiences.

Writing a Letter to Your Past Self

This involves writing a letter to a younger version of you who experienced pain or hurt. You might want to reassure your past self, offer them the wisdom you've gained since then, or simply acknowledge the hurt they went through.

Writing a Letter to Your Current Self

This can be a letter of encouragement, acknowledging the steps you're taking to heal and reinforcing your strength and resilience. It could also be a self-compassionate letter, treating your current self with kindness and understanding.

Writing a Letter to Someone Else

This might be a letter to someone who has caused you hurt. The goal isn't necessarily to send this letter (and in many cases, it's better not to), but to express the feelings that you've been holding onto. This can help you to let go of lingering anger or resentment.

Remember, these letters are for you. You don't have to share them with anyone. Be honest and allow yourself to feel whatever emotions arise. It's all part of the healing process.

Chapter 7: Embracing Imperfections

Defining Perfectionism

Perfectionism is a complex personality trait that is characterized by setting exceedingly high standards for performance and a tendency to make overly critical self-evaluations. It's not just about setting and striving for ambitious goals, but it's tied to a deep-seated fear of failure or making mistakes. This fear can lead to extreme behaviors and thought patterns, such as spending excessive amounts of time on tasks to ensure they are done perfectly, avoiding new tasks or opportunities for fear of not being able to do them perfectly, or experiencing severe stress and anxiety over minor mistakes or imperfections.

The Dual Nature of Perfectionism

While perfectionism is often seen as a negative trait due to its association with stress, anxiety, and other mental health issues, it can also have positive aspects. Striving for high standards can lead to impressive achievements, and attention to detail can increase quality in many areas of life. The key is to distinguish between healthy striving for excellence and harmful perfectionism that leads to self-criticism and stress. Understanding this difference is crucial in learning how to manage perfectionist tendencies effectively.

The Unrealistic Expectations of Perfection

Perfection, by its nature, is an unrealistic goal. No human being is without flaws or makes no mistakes. Yet, perfectionists often hold themselves to this unattainable standard. This is not only unrealistic but also harmful, as it leads to constant feelings of dissatisfaction, disappointment, and self-criticism. Recognizing the unrealistic nature of perfection is an important step towards developing self-love and self-acceptance.

Embracing Imperfection as a Part of Being Human

Imperfections, mistakes, and flaws are a natural part of being human. Each one of us has unique quirks and characteristics that make us who we are. When we learn to accept and even embrace these imperfections, we can develop a more compassionate and loving view of ourselves. We can also reduce the stress and anxiety associated with striving for perfection and enjoy a more balanced and fulfilling life.

The Impact of Perfectionism on Self-Love

Perfectionism can pose a significant barrier to self-love. If we're constantly striving for perfection, we may never feel good enough, and we may neglect to appreciate our accomplishments and positive qualities. This can lead to negative self-talk and lower self-esteem, hindering our ability to love and accept ourselves.

Overcoming Perfectionism

Overcoming perfectionism doesn't mean letting go of all standards or stop striving to do your best. Instead, it involves recognizing when our standards are unreasonably high and adjusting them to be more realistic and compassionate. It also involves changing the way we respond to perceived failures and mistakes, treating ourselves with kindness and understanding instead of harsh self-criticism.

Embracing Imperfections

Embracing imperfections is about more than just accepting that we have flaws; it's about recognizing that these flaws make us who we are. Our imperfections, mistakes, and failures can provide opportunities for learning and growth. They can make us more empathetic and understanding towards others. And they can help us to appreciate our achievements and progress, knowing how hard we've worked and how far we've come.

Self-Reflective Activity

Activity 1: Identifying Perfectionist Tendencies

The first step to managing perfectionism is to recognize it. Reflect on your habits, thought patterns, and behaviors. Do you often strive for flawless performance? Do you tend to be excessively critical of your mistakes? Do you avoid new experiences or tasks out of fear of not doing them perfectly?

This activity involves journaling about situations where you have displayed perfectionist tendencies. Detail the situation, how you reacted, and the thoughts and feelings associated with it.

Activity 2: Challenging Unrealistic Standards

Now that you've identified your perfectionist tendencies, the next step is to challenge them. Look at the situations you journaled about. What standards or expectations were you holding yourself to? Were they reasonable or unrealistic? Could you have done a 'good enough' job and still achieved your goal?

This activity asks you to challenge the standards you set in each situation and come up with more realistic and compassionate expectations.

Activity 3: Embracing Imperfections

This activity aims to help you develop a more positive relationship with your imperfections. List some of your imperfections or mistakes you've made and then write down something positive about them. For example, if you made a mistake in a project, the positive side might be that you learned something new, or it gave you an opportunity to improve.

Remember, this is a process, and it's okay if you find these exercises challenging at first. The aim is not to eliminate perfectionism overnight but to gradually shift your perspective and embrace a more self-compassionate approach.

Embracing Imperfections and Striving for Progress

Embracing imperfections and striving for progress rather than perfection requires a shift in mindset. This starts with recognizing and accepting that perfection is an unrealistic standard. Instead, focus on progress. Ask yourself: "Am I better today than I was yesterday?" even if the improvement is small, it's still progress.

Part of this journey involves treating mistakes and failures as opportunities to learn and grow, not as indicators of worthlessness or incompetence. Changing your self-talk can also be a powerful tool in this process. Instead of saying "I must do this perfectly," try saying "I will do my best, and that is enough."

Remember, self-love and self-acceptance are about recognizing and appreciating your worth, despite (and because of) your imperfections. It's about acknowledging your strengths and embracing your weaknesses. It's about making peace with who you are, as you are.

Activity - Challenging Perfectionist Thoughts

This activity aims to help you change your perfectionist thinking patterns. It's a two-part exercise:

Part 1: Recognize Perfectionist Thoughts

Write down any thoughts you've had recently that involve perfectionism. These could be thoughts like, "If I can't do it perfectly, there's no point in doing it at all," or "I must not make a mistake."

Part 2: Challenge and Replace Perfectionist Thoughts

Now, take each thought and challenge it. Is it realistic? Is it helpful? What evidence do you have that this thought is true? Next, try to replace each perfectionist thought with a more balanced and rational thought. For example, you could replace "I must not make a mistake" with "Everyone makes mistakes; they're opportunities to learn."

The goal of this exercise is to help you develop a healthier, more balanced perspective on perfectionism and to cultivate a more compassionate internal dialogue. It's okay if this feels difficult at first; with practice, it will become easier.

Chapter 8: Building Resilience

Resilience is a vital component of self-love. It refers to our capacity to recover from difficulties, to adapt well in the face of adversity, trauma, tragedy, or significant sources of stress. Resilience allows us to withstand and bounce back from life's challenges, and it can be cultivated and strengthened with practice.

The Importance of Resilience in Self-Love

Resilience is closely tied to self-love. When we love ourselves, we are better able to face challenges without losing our sense of self-worth or falling into negative self-talk. Similarly, resilience allows us to navigate through difficult times without losing our sense of self-love.

Resilience is especially important because life will inevitably present us with challenges and difficulties. Whether it's the end of a relationship, the loss of a job, or any other significant life change, these challenges can test our self-love. When we're resilient, we can face these tests with strength and grace, maintaining our self-love even in the face of adversity.

Resilient people do not ignore the pain or pretend everything is okay; instead, they recognize the struggle, and they work through the pain while maintaining a positive outlook. They understand that setbacks are temporary and that they have the strength and resources to overcome adversity.

By building resilience, we can ensure that our self-love is not contingent on things always going smoothly. We can continue to love ourselves through the ups and downs of life, knowing that we have the strength to weather any storm. This chapter will provide tools and strategies to build and enhance resilience, strengthening your self-love in the process.

Tools and Techniques to Build Resilience

Building resilience is a process that involves several strategies, including cultivating a positive mindset, strengthening your problem-solving skills, maintaining healthy relationships, and taking care of your physical health. Here are some tools and techniques:

1. **Positive Mindset:** Cultivating a positive mindset involves practicing optimism and gratitude. Positive thinking doesn't mean ignoring the reality of difficult situations, but it does involve seeking out the positive aspects and maintaining hope for better outcomes.
2. **Mindfulness and Emotional Awareness:** Practicing mindfulness can help you respond to stress more effectively by focusing on the present moment without judgment. It also enhances your emotional awareness, enabling you to recognize and manage your feelings more effectively.
3. **Problem-Solving Skills:** Developing problem-solving skills can increase your sense of control over the

situations you encounter. When faced with a challenge, rather than getting overwhelmed, you can take a step back, assess the situation, and devise a plan.

4. **Healthy Relationships:** Maintaining strong, supportive relationships can provide a cushion in times of stress. Cultivate relationships that offer emotional support, practical help, and guidance when you need it.

5. **Physical Health:** Regular exercise, a balanced diet, and adequate sleep can all improve your resilience. They boost your mood, provide energy, and enhance your overall sense of wellbeing, enabling you to face challenges more effectively.

6. **Self-Care:** Regular self-care is a crucial part of building resilience. This includes taking time to relax, engage in hobbies or activities you enjoy, and giving yourself permission to take breaks and recharge.

7. **Setting Realistic Goals:** Setting and working towards realistic goals can build your confidence and resilience over time. It provides a sense of purpose and direction, which can help when facing adversity.

8. **Professional Help:** Sometimes, it can be beneficial to seek professional help, like a psychologist or a counselor, to learn more effective strategies for building resilience. This can be particularly helpful if you're going through a challenging time or have a history of significant adversity.

In the following sections of the chapter, these techniques will be expanded upon, with practical tips and activities for each.

Remember, building resilience is a process, not a one-time task. It's okay to take small steps and gradually incorporate these strategies into your life. Every step you take towards building resilience is a step towards strengthening your self-love.

Activity - Developing a Resilience Action Plan

A resilience action plan is a personal guide that helps you to identify and leverage your strengths while acknowledging areas that need growth. It can serve as a blueprint to handle stress, adversity, or change in a healthy and adaptive way. Here's a step-by-step guide on how to develop your own resilience action plan:

1. **Identify Stressors:** Start by identifying the primary stressors in your life. These could be related to work, personal relationships, health, or any other aspect that causes significant stress.
2. **Assess Your Current Resilience Skills:** Reflect on how you usually handle these stressors. What strategies have you used in the past? Have they been effective or not? This can help you understand what aspects of resilience you're already strong in and what areas might need improvement.
3. **Identify Growth Areas:** From the resilience-building tools mentioned above (positive mindset, mindfulness, problem-solving skills, healthy relationships, physical health, self-care, setting realistic goals, and seeking

professional help), choose two or three areas you'd like to focus on to improve your resilience.

4. **Develop Action Steps:** For each of the areas you've chosen to focus on, identify specific actions you can take to enhance your resilience. For example, if you choose to focus on 'positive mindset,' an action step might be to practice daily gratitude by jotting down three things you're grateful for each day.

5. **Identify Supports:** Resilience doesn't have to be a solo journey. Consider who or what might support you in your resilience-building journey. This could include friends, family, a mentor, a support group, or a mental health professional.

6. **Set a Review Date:** Change takes time, and so does building resilience. Set a review date for a few weeks or months in the future to reassess your progress. At that point, you can reflect on what's working, what isn't, and adjust your plan accordingly.

7. **Commit to Your Plan:** The last step is to make a commitment to yourself to follow your resilience action plan. Remember, the goal isn't to achieve perfection, but to make progress.

Remember, this action plan is flexible. It's okay to make changes as you progress and as your needs and circumstances evolve. Building resilience is a journey, and this action plan is your map. However, just like any journey, the route can be adjusted as needed

Chapter 9: The Role of Forgiveness in Self-Love

The Power of Forgiveness

Forgiveness is a significant and impactful aspect of self-love. It's about releasing resentment and finding peace, freeing ourselves from the bonds of anger and bitterness. Forgiveness isn't about excusing or forgetting hurtful behaviors; instead, it's about reducing the hold these experiences have over us.

When we forgive others, we allow ourselves to let go of the emotional baggage attached to past wrongs. It can liberate us from the cycle of negativity and allow us to move forward with our lives with greater peace and positivity.

Equally important is the act of self-forgiveness. As humans, we are not perfect and are prone to make mistakes. However, dwelling on these mistakes, feeling guilty, and blaming ourselves does not contribute to our wellbeing or growth. Self-forgiveness is about accepting our flaws and failures, learning from them, and moving forward. It is about treating ourselves with the same kindness and understanding we would offer to others.

The Process of Forgiveness

Forgiveness is a journey, not a destination, and it typically involves several key stages:

1. Acknowledgment: The first step in the process of forgiveness is acknowledging the hurt. It's important to be honest about how you feel and not downplay or ignore the hurt just to maintain the peace. Allow yourself to feel the pain without judgement or trying to rush the healing process.

2. Understanding: Try to understand why the person may have acted the way they did. This does not mean you are justifying their actions, but understanding can lead to empathy, which is a powerful step towards forgiveness.

3. Empathy: Empathy involves trying to see things from the other person's perspective. It doesn't mean you agree with them, but understanding their point of view can help you process your emotions and possibly lessen the pain.

4. Decision: Deciding to forgive is a crucial step. Forgiveness is a conscious choice that you make for your peace of mind and wellbeing.

5. Release: Let go of resentment and thoughts of revenge. Holding onto these negative feelings only continues to hurt you. By releasing them, you make space for more positive emotions and experiences.

6. Healing: Once you decide to forgive and let go of the past, the healing process begins. This does not mean that you forget the hurtful event, but you choose not to let it control your life anymore.

7. Future: Forgiveness allows you to move forward with your life, focusing on the present and future instead of being stuck in the past. This contributes to a healthier, happier future.

The process of forgiveness is not linear and each person's journey is unique. It's okay if it takes time and patience. Sometimes, it may help to seek support from a therapist or counselor to guide you through this process.

Benefits of Forgiveness

Forgiveness is more than just an act of kindness towards the person who hurt you; it can also have substantial benefits for your own physical and mental health:

1. **Healthier Relationships:** Forgiveness can mend bridges and lead to healthier, stronger relationships. It can clear the air, restore trust, and foster understanding, leading to more profound connections.
2. **Improved Mental Health:** Forgiveness is closely linked to lower levels of depression, anxiety, and symptoms of post-traumatic stress disorder (PTSD). When we forgive,

we let go of the heavy burden of resentment and anger, which can significantly alleviate emotional distress.

3. **Reduced Stress and Anxiety:** By releasing grudges and resentment, we can lower the level of stress and anxiety in our lives. Constantly dwelling on negative past events can keep us in a state of chronic stress and high anxiety.

4. **Lower Blood Pressure and Improved Heart Health:** Holding onto anger and resentment can increase blood pressure and heart rate. On the contrary, forgiveness can lead to lower blood pressure and a reduced risk of heart disease.

5. **Stronger Immune System:** Mental and emotional health can significantly impact our physical health, including the immune system. Reduced stress and emotional distress associated with forgiveness can boost our immunity.

6. **Decreased Depression:** Forgiveness, particularly self-forgiveness, can be a powerful tool against symptoms of depression.

7. **Increased Self-esteem and Self-love:** Holding onto guilt, shame, and resentment, especially towards oneself, can damage self-esteem. Forgiveness allows us to let go of these negative feelings and replace them with understanding and self-compassion, leading to increased self-love.

Remember, forgiveness is a personal journey that looks different for everyone. It's a gift you give to yourself, paving the way for peace, happiness, and wellbeing.

Forgiveness and Self-Love

Forgiveness is a critical aspect of self-love and self-care. By holding onto resentment, guilt, or anger, we keep ourselves trapped in a cycle of negative emotions that can affect our sense of self-worth and our ability to experience joy and fulfillment.

When we talk about forgiveness, it's crucial to consider two facets - forgiving others and forgiving ourselves. Both are equally important for cultivating self-love.

Forgiving Others: Holding onto resentment or anger towards others can be draining. It keeps us anchored to the past, preventing us from moving forward. By forgiving others, we release ourselves from this burden. It doesn't mean we forget what happened or condone the action; instead, we decide not to let it control our emotions anymore. This act of letting go can provide a sense of peace and empowerment that significantly contributes to our capacity for self-love.

Self-Forgiveness: Self-forgiveness is perhaps even more critical to self-love. We all make mistakes, but it's essential to remember that mistakes don't define our worth. Self-forgiveness involves acknowledging our faults, learning from them, and then letting them go. It means treating ourselves with the same compassion and understanding we'd offer to a loved one who made a mistake.

By forgiving ourselves, we affirm that we are more than our missteps. We learn to focus on our growth, our capacity for change, and our inherent worth. This ability to acknowledge our mistakes without devaluing ourselves fuels self-love and opens the path to self-improvement and personal growth.

As such, forgiveness, both of others and ourselves, is a powerful tool in our self-love journey. It allows us to release negativity and create space for understanding, compassion, and acceptance - for others and, most importantly, for ourselves.

Self-Reflective Activity: Journey to Forgiveness

This section of the workbook is dedicated to self-reflective activities that aim to facilitate your personal journey towards forgiveness. The intention is to guide you in letting go of resentment, bitterness, and negative feelings that you may be holding onto, which are impeding your journey to self-love. These activities may bring up some challenging emotions, but remember, it's all part of the healing process.

Identifying Areas for Forgiveness: The first step is to identify areas in your life where forgiveness is needed. This could include moments when you feel you have been wronged by others or instances where you feel guilt or regret over your actions. Recognizing these instances is crucial in understanding what emotions and experiences you need to work through.

Writing Forgiveness Letters: Writing can be a powerful tool in the process of forgiveness. You will be guided to write letters of forgiveness to others and to yourself. The purpose of this exercise isn't necessarily to send these letters, but to help you articulate your feelings and facilitate the process of letting go. Remember, forgiveness is more about your healing than the person who has hurt you.

Forgiveness Meditations: Lastly, you will be guided through forgiveness meditations. These exercises will help you cultivate a mindset of compassion, understanding, and forgiveness. They can be repeated as often as needed, each time aiming to bring you closer to a state of forgiveness and self-love.

As you undertake these exercises, remember that forgiveness is a journey, not a destination. It's perfectly okay if you find it hard to forgive at first. With time, patience, and continuous practice, you'll make progress. The goal of these exercises is to aid in that progression and to guide you on your path towards deeper self-love.

Steps Toward Forgiveness

Forgiving isn't always easy; in fact, it can be a long, emotional journey that takes considerable time and patience. However, the benefits are significant as it contributes to improved mental, emotional, and physical wellbeing, not to mention fostering a deeper sense of self-love. Here are some steps to guide you in your journey towards forgiveness:

1. Acknowledge the Hurt: The first step towards forgiveness is acknowledging the hurt. It's essential to validate your feelings and admit to yourself that you were hurt by someone's actions or words. Denying the pain only prolongs the healing process.

2. Express Your Feelings: Once you've acknowledged the hurt, it's important to express those feelings, either privately in a journal, through art, in conversation with a trusted friend or therapist, or even towards the person who hurt you if you feel it's appropriate and safe.

3. Try to Understand: In instances where someone else has hurt you, try to see things from their perspective. This doesn't mean you condone their behavior, but understanding their motivations or circumstances can often make it easier to forgive. If the person you need to forgive is yourself, try to understand why you acted the way you did and show compassion towards yourself.

4. Make the Decision to Forgive: Forgiveness is a choice. Make a conscious decision to let go of resentment and anger towards the person who hurt you, or towards yourself. Remember, forgiveness is more for your peace of mind than it is for the other person.

5. Practice Empathy and Compassion: Try to empathize with the person who hurt you, and show compassion towards them. If it's self-forgiveness you're seeking, direct that empathy and compassion towards yourself.

6. Let Go and Move Forward: Once you've worked through the previous steps, it's time to let go of the hurt and resentment, and move forward. This doesn't mean you forget the hurt or allow yourself to be hurt again; it simply means that you're not allowing the past to negatively affect your present and future.

Remember, these steps aren't necessarily linear and you might find yourself looping back to earlier steps during your journey towards forgiveness. That's completely okay. Healing isn't a straight path, but with persistence and patience, you'll make progress.

Activity: Forgiveness Meditation

Meditation can be a helpful tool in the process of forgiveness, as it provides a calm and focused space to work through complex emotions. Here's a step-by-step guide to a forgiveness meditation:

Step 1: Find a Quiet Space: Choose a calm and quiet space where you won't be disturbed. It can be a specific room in your house, your garden, or even a park. The key is to find a location where you feel peaceful and can focus your mind.

Step 2: Get Comfortable: Find a comfortable sitting position. It can be on a chair, on a cushion on the floor, or even lying down. The important thing is that you're comfortable and your spine is in a neutral position.

Step 3: Begin With Deep Breathing: Close your eyes and begin by taking a few deep breaths. Breathe in through your nose, hold it for a few seconds, and then exhale through your mouth. Concentrate on your breath as it moves in and out of your body.

Step 4: Visualize the Person: Once you're relaxed, bring to mind the person you want to forgive or the situation where you felt hurt. If you're working on self-forgiveness, visualize yourself in the situation.

Step 5: Acknowledge the Hurt: As you visualize, allow yourself to acknowledge the hurt or anger you felt. Validate these feelings, but try to do so without judgement. It's okay to feel hurt or angry.

Step 6: Express Forgiveness: Now, express your forgiveness towards this person or towards yourself. You might say something like, "I forgive you for the pain you've caused me" or "I forgive myself for my past mistakes." You can say this silently in your mind or out loud, whichever feels more natural to you.

Step 7: Release the Hurt: Visualize the hurt and anger you've been holding onto melting away or being released into the universe. Feel the weight being lifted from your heart.

Step 8: End the Meditation: After you've spent some time releasing the hurt, slowly bring your awareness back to your surroundings. Notice the surface you're sitting or lying on, the sounds around you, and finally, when you're ready, open your eyes.

Remember, forgiveness doesn't always come easily or immediately. If you don't feel ready to forgive after the first meditation, that's okay. It's a process. You can return to this meditation as often as you need. Also, it's normal to feel a wide range of emotions during and after the meditation. Consider journaling about your experience afterward to process these feelings.

Chapter 10: Cultivating Gratitude

The Connection Between Gratitude and Self-Love

Gratitude is a powerful emotion that can significantly enhance our sense of self-love. It encourages us to focus on the positive aspects of our lives, thereby promoting feelings of happiness, contentment, and well-being. When we express gratitude, we acknowledge the goodness in our lives and, as a result, positive feelings flourish.

Gratitude and self-love are closely linked because when we appreciate the positive aspects of our lives, we are also acknowledging our worth and the value we bring to the world. This sense of self-worth is a crucial element of self-love.

When we practice gratitude regularly, we become more attuned to the positive aspects of our lives, rather than focusing on our perceived flaws or shortcomings. This shift in focus can help improve our self-esteem, increase our sense of self-worth, and lead to a stronger sense of self-love.

By learning to appreciate what we have, who we are, and our experiences (both good and bad), we cultivate a sense of contentment and acceptance of ourselves as we are, which is the essence of self-love.

Throughout this chapter, we'll explore different strategies and activities for incorporating gratitude into your daily routine to enhance your journey toward self-love.

Techniques to Cultivate a Regular Gratitude Practice

Cultivating a regular gratitude practice can be a transformative way to foster self-love. Below are several techniques that can help you make gratitude a daily habit:

1. **Gratitude Journal:** A popular way to cultivate gratitude is by keeping a gratitude journal. Each day, write down three things you're grateful for. They don't have to be big things—sometimes, it's the small things in life that bring us the most joy.

2. **Gratitude Jar:** Another way to cultivate gratitude is by creating a gratitude jar. Each day, write something you're grateful for on a piece of paper and put it in the jar. Over time, you'll accumulate a jar full of positive thoughts and experiences. When you're feeling down, you can reach into your jar for a quick pick-me-up.

3. **Gratitude Letters:** Writing letters of gratitude to the people who have positively impacted your life is another powerful way to cultivate gratitude. These letters don't necessarily need to be sent—you could write them for your own reflection. However, sharing your gratitude can often amplify its benefits.

4. **Mindful Gratitude Practices:** Incorporating gratitude into mindfulness practices, such as meditation or yoga, can also be beneficial. For example, during meditation, you could focus on something you're grateful for, holding it in your mind as you breathe in and out.

5. **Gratitude Reminders:** Set reminders on your phone or computer to pause and consider something you're grateful for. This could be a moment of calm during a busy day and a valuable tool for reframing negative thoughts.

6. **Gratitude Prompts:** Use gratitude prompts to help you think of new things to be grateful for. Prompts could be simple statements or questions like, "Today I appreciated..." or "What made me smile today was..."

Remember, there's no right or wrong way to practice gratitude. The key is to find a practice that fits into your life and feels right for you. It might feel awkward at first, but with time, you'll likely start to notice a shift in your mood and overall outlook on life.

Activity: Gratitude Journaling

Gratitude journaling is an effective practice for cultivating gratitude and, in turn, enhancing self-love. It allows us to focus on the positive aspects of our lives, no matter how big or small they may be. Here's a simple step-by-step guide to start your own gratitude journaling practice:

1. **Choose Your Journal:** Your gratitude journal can be a physical notebook, a digital document, or even an app specifically designed for gratitude journaling. Choose what feels the most comfortable for you.
2. **Set a Routine:** Decide on a specific time each day to write in your gratitude journal. It could be in the morning to start your day positively, or in the evening before bed to reflect on the day's events. Regularity is key for this practice to become a habit.
3. **Write Down What You're Grateful For:** Every day, write down three things you're grateful for. They can be simple things like a beautiful sunrise, a good cup of coffee, or a phone call with a friend. Try to be as specific as possible, and focus on people or experiences rather than material possessions.
4. **Reflect on Your Feelings:** After writing down what you're grateful for, spend a moment reflecting on how these things made you feel. This can deepen your sense of gratitude.
5. **Read Back Through Your Entries:** Every once in a while, read back through your previous entries. This can

be a great boost on difficult days, reminding you of the positive things in your life.

Remember, there's no wrong way to keep a gratitude journal. It's a personal practice, and what matters most is that it helps you cultivate a greater sense of gratitude and self-love.

Chapter 11: Nurturing Healthy Relationships

Identifying Healthy vs. Unhealthy Relationships

Recognizing the difference between healthy and unhealthy relationships is critical to our well-being and self-love. Healthy relationships are characterized by mutual respect, open communication, trust, equality, and freedom. Unhealthy relationships, on the other hand, may involve manipulation, control, secrecy, disrespect, or abuse.

In healthy relationships:

- There's open, honest, and respectful communication. Each person feels heard and valued.
- Both individuals feel free to express their needs and desires without fear of criticism or retaliation.
- There's a balance of power and control. Decisions are made jointly, and each person has an equal say.
- Each person respects the other's individuality, is supportive of the other's growth and independence, and takes responsibility for their actions.

Unhealthy relationships can be marked by:

- Disrespect or manipulation.
- Poor communication, including withholding information, lying, or the inability to have open conversations.

- Control or dominance by one person over the other.
- Dependency or co-dependency.
- Lack of support for the other person's interests or goals.

Understanding these differences can help you evaluate the relationships in your life, making changes or seeking help if necessary. It also guides you in building and maintaining healthier relationships moving forward. Healthy relationships are essential in nurturing self-love, as they reflect the respect and value you have for yourself.

Techniques for Nurturing Relationships that Foster Self-Love

Nurturing relationships that foster self-love requires intentional actions and continuous effort. Here are some techniques:

1. **Establish and Maintain Boundaries**: Boundaries define what is acceptable and what isn't in your relationships. They're crucial for maintaining self-respect and ensuring that your relationships are mutually respectful and fulfilling.
2. **Communicate Openly and Honestly**: Open, honest communication builds trust and understanding. It's important to express your feelings, needs, and concerns clearly and respectfully.
3. **Practice Active Listening**: Active listening involves truly hearing and understanding the other person's point of view. It shows respect and validation, fostering deeper connections.

4. **Show Appreciation and Gratitude**: Regularly expressing appreciation and gratitude can strengthen bonds and foster positivity in your relationships. It helps others feel valued and loved.

5. **Invest Time and Effort**: Relationships require time and effort to grow and strengthen. Regularly spend quality time with your loved ones, be there for them in times of need, and invest in shared experiences.

6. **Encourage and Support Each Other's Growth**: A relationship that fosters self-love is one where both parties support and encourage each other's personal growth and individuality.

7. **Seek and Give Respect**: In any relationship, respect is paramount. It includes respecting each other's choices, opinions, boundaries, and individuality.

8. **Practice Forgiveness**: Holding on to grudges or past hurts can harm relationships. Practicing forgiveness allows for healing and the continuation of a healthy relationship.

Remember, it's important to nurture relationships that positively contribute to your journey of self-love. Unhealthy or toxic relationships can hinder your growth and impact your self-esteem.

Activity - Relationship Mapping

Relationship Mapping is an activity designed to help you evaluate the various relationships in your life and how they impact your journey of self-love. It can aid you in recognizing the relationships that nurture your growth and those that might be hindering it. Here's a step-by-step guide to perform this activity:

Step 1: Identify Your Relationships Write down the names of the people who are part of your life. This list should include family, friends, coworkers, romantic partners, and anyone else who plays a significant role in your day-to-day life.

Step 2: Evaluate Each Relationship Next to each name, write a brief description of how that person affects your self-esteem and self-love. Does their presence uplift you, or does it drain your energy? Are they supportive and respectful of your boundaries, or do they overstep or disregard them?

Step 3: Categorize The Relationships Based on your evaluations, categorize these relationships into those that are positive, neutral, or negative. Positive relationships contribute to your self-love and personal growth, neutral ones don't significantly affect it one way or another, and negative ones hinder your self-love journey.

Step 4: Reflect Reflect on your relationship map. Are there more positive relationships than negative ones? Are there relationships that need work? Are there people you need to spend more time with or people you should distance yourself from?

Step 5: Action Plan Create an action plan based on your reflections. This might involve setting boundaries with some people, investing more time in others, or making efforts to transform neutral relationships into positive ones.

Remember, this exercise isn't about cutting people out of your life; it's about becoming aware of how different relationships affect your self-love journey and making necessary adjustments to nurture your well-being.

Incorporating Self-Love into Daily Life

Practicing self-love is an ongoing journey, not a one-time event. It is something you nurture and cultivate each day. Here's how you can incorporate self-love into your daily life:

1. Start Your Day with Self-Love: Begin each day with a positive affirmation or self-love ritual that sets a positive tone for the day. This could be a few moments of meditation, a positive affirmation, or writing in a gratitude journal.

2. Practice Mindfulness: Stay aware of your thoughts and feelings throughout the day. When negative thoughts arise, recognize them, challenge them, and try to replace them with more positive or neutral thoughts.

3. Set and Respect Boundaries: Protect your time, energy, and emotional well-being by setting and respecting personal boundaries. This might involve saying no when you need to, taking time for self-care, or distancing yourself from negativity.

4. Practice Self-Care: Regularly take time to care for your physical, emotional, and mental health. This might involve physical exercise, healthy eating, meditation, relaxation activities, or engaging in hobbies and activities you enjoy.

5. Stay Connected with Supportive People: Nurture relationships with people who uplift you, respect your boundaries, and support your journey of self-love.

6. Practice Forgiveness: Forgive yourself and others for past mistakes and hurts. Forgiveness is a powerful act of self-love that allows you to let go of negativity and move forward.

7. Celebrate Yourself: Recognize your accomplishments, however small they may seem. Celebrating yourself boosts self-esteem and reinforces the love you have for yourself.

Remember, living a life of self-love is a journey, not a destination. Some days may be harder than others, and that's okay. Be gentle with yourself and take each day as it comes. You are deserving of love, especially from yourself.

Maintaining Self-Love During Difficult Times

Maintaining self-love can be especially challenging during difficult times, but it's also when you need it the most. Here are some strategies you can use to nurture self-love even in the face of adversity:

1. Practice Self-Compassion: Be kind to yourself when you're going through a hard time. Acknowledge your feelings without judgement and give yourself the same compassion you'd give to a friend in a similar situation.

2. Stay Connected: Reach out to supportive friends, family members, or a mental health professional. You don't have to go through difficult times alone, and sharing your feelings with others can help lighten your emotional load.

3. Prioritize Self-Care: It's easy to neglect self-care when you're facing challenges, but this is when it's most important. Make sure to eat well, get plenty of rest, engage in regular physical activity, and take time to do things that help you relax and recharge.

4. Engage in Mindfulness Practices: Mindfulness can help you stay grounded and focused on the present moment, which can be particularly helpful during difficult times. This could be in the form of meditation, yoga, or simply taking a few moments each day to breathe deeply and intentionally.

5. Reinforce Positive Self-Talk: Negative self-talk can increase during hard times. Be aware of your internal dialogue and consciously work on shifting negative thoughts to more positive ones.

6. Seek Professional Help: If you're finding it really hard to maintain self-love and are feeling overwhelmed, don't hesitate to seek help from a mental health professional. They can provide strategies and techniques to help you navigate through your challenges.

Remember, it's perfectly okay to have bad days and it's okay to ask for help. You're human, and dealing with difficult times is part of the human experience. Treat yourself with kindness and patience as you navigate these times.

Celebration of the Journey Towards Self-Love

The journey towards self-love is not an easy one; it's filled with ups and downs, moments of revelation, and times of struggle. It involves unlearning negative patterns, healing old wounds, and embracing oneself fully, including the imperfections. But every step you take in this journey is a reason for celebration.

1. Acknowledge Progress: It's crucial to acknowledge your progress, no matter how small it might seem. Celebrate the fact that you are making an effort to love yourself, that you're working on establishing healthier habits and relationships, and that you're actively trying to heal.

2. Be Proud of Your Courage: It takes courage to face our insecurities and fears, to dig deep into past wounds, and to challenge the status quo. Be proud of the courage you've shown throughout this journey.

3. Reflect on Your Growth: Take some time to reflect on your growth. Think about where you started and where you are now. Recognize the strength, resilience, and patience you've shown along the way.

4. Practice Gratitude: As you celebrate your journey towards self-love, don't forget to practice gratitude. Be grateful for the journey itself and all the lessons it has taught you.

5. Treat Yourself: Lastly, don't forget to treat yourself. Do something that makes you feel good. It could be a pampering session, a leisurely walk, a special meal, or simply some quiet time to relax.

The journey towards self-love is an ongoing one. There will always be more to learn and ways to grow. Keep in mind that the goal is not to achieve a perfect state of self-love, but to continuously work towards loving yourself more each day. So, celebrate your journey and all the little victories along the way. You are worth it!